EMPIRE IN POWER

CONTENTS

INTRODUCTION

Although the dark side's Empire rules supreme, the forces of good still rise to oppose it. Those who remember the time of the Republic and the Jedi join forces as the Rebel Alliance, and swear to end the Emperor's reign and restore peace and justice to the galaxy.

Darth Sidious cannot allow such insolence. He orders his loyal apprentice Darth Vader to hunt down the rebels and find their hidden bases. And to finish the job, he prepares to use a devastating secret weapon that has been many years in the building…

THE ABILITY TO DESTROY A PLANET IS... ACTUALLY PRETTY IMPRESSIVE, WHEN YOU THINK ABOUT IT.

EMPLOYEE OF THE MONTH
Emperor Palpatine is a very demanding boss. Palpatine once gave Vader a medal for doing a great job… but he soon took it away after Vader accidentally knocked over a battalion of stormtroopers!

Blade powered by crimson crystal

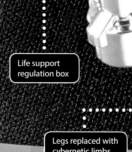

DARTH VADER

FEW WHO MEET him would believe that Darth Vader was once a noble Jedi Knight. He is short-tempered, destructive, and cruel, with a strength and rage that are feared by his enemies and allies alike. Even his Imperial underlings avoid him, because to anger Lord Vader is to face doom.

Life support regulation box

Legs replaced with cybernetic limbs

MILITARY COMMANDER

As the Emperor's military enforcer, Vader commands entire fleets of mighty Star Destroyers in battle. Squadrons of TIE fighters follow his orders, which are most effective when Vader leads in his personal starfighter. His tactical skills make him especially fearsome when hunting fugitive rebels and Jedi.

DARK LORD

Vader serves as the right-hand man to Emperor Palpatine, who rules the entire Empire of millions of planets and star systems. His duties are to carry out the Emperor's will, enforce the harsh Imperial laws throughout the galaxy, and wipe out any Jedi that he can find.

> ❝ YOU DON'T KNOW THE POWER OF THE DARK SIDE. ❞
>
> DARTH VADER

DATA FILE

- **HOMEWORLD:** TATOOINE
- **BIRTH DATE:** 41 BBY
- **RANK:** SITH LORD
- **TRAINED BY:** OBI-WAN KENOBI, DARTH SIDIOUS
- **WEAPON:** RED-BLADED LIGHTSABER

THE PATH TO THE DARK SIDE

Anakin Skywalker started out a hero, but his uncontrolled emotions and selfish choices led him to become a Dark Lord of the Sith. His journey to evil was complete when his face and body were sealed inside his black mask and armor.

THE MAN IN THE MASK

DARTH VADER'S MASK and armor cover his entire body. They contain many high-tech mechanisms that keep him alive—and their appearance also intimidates his enemies! Underneath the durasteel plating and padded body suit, cybernetic systems are wired directly into Vader's body, letting him move as if he still had his original limbs.

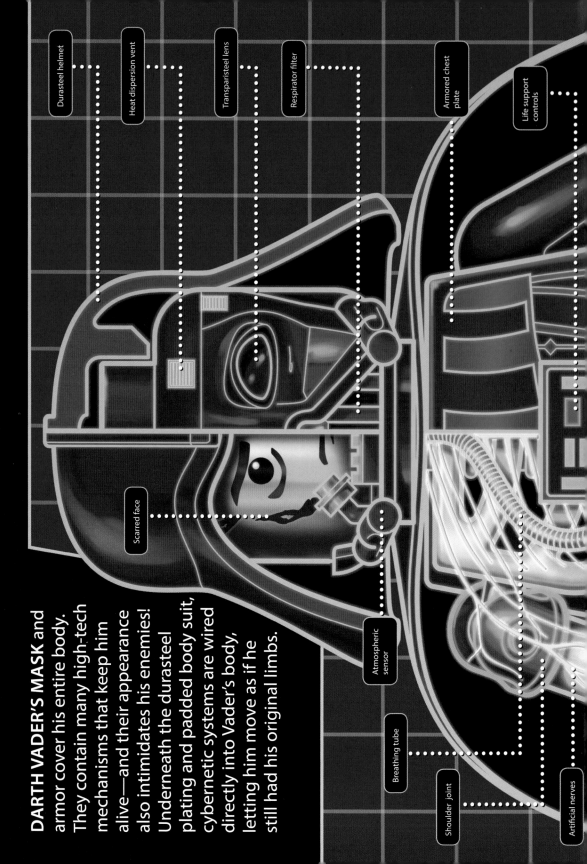

Durasteel helmet

Heat dispersion vent

Transparisteel lens

Respirator filter

Armored chest plate

Life support controls

Scarred face

Atmospheric sensor

Breathing tube

Shoulder joint

Artificial nerves

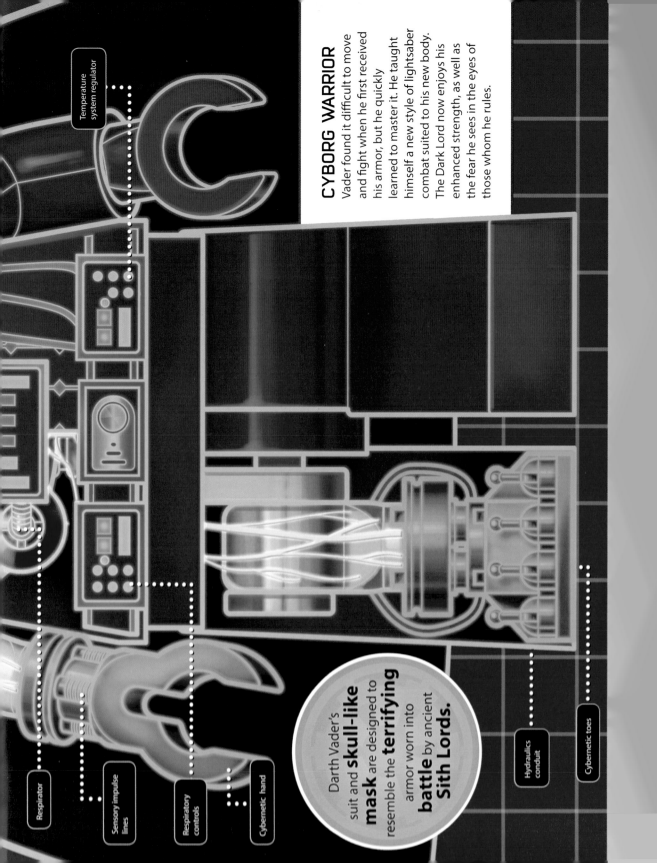

CYBORG WARRIOR

Vader found it difficult to move and fight when he first received his armor, but he quickly learned to master it. He taught himself a new style of lightsaber combat suited to his new body. The Dark Lord now enjoys his enhanced strength, as well as the fear he sees in the eyes of those whom he rules.

Temperature system regulator

Darth Vader's suit and **skull-like mask** are designed to resemble the **terrifying battle** armor worn by ancient **Sith Lords.**

Respirator

Sensory impulse lines

Respiratory controls

Cybernetic hand

Hydraulics conduit

Cybernetic toes

IMPERIAL FORCES

AFTER MORE THAN 25,000 years, the Republic is no more—long live the Galactic Empire! With Darth Vader as the Emperor's enforcer, the new order rules with an iron fist, crushing any world that dares to resist. A vast army of stormtroopers and technology help the Empire maintain control over the galaxy.

IMPERIAL INVASION

The Empire believes in overwhelming its enemies through superior numbers and firepower. When Darth Vader discovers a rebel base on the ice planet Hoth, he sends in a squad of mechanized AT-ATs (All Terrain Armored Transports) to annihilate it.

> BRRR! IT'S A CHILLY JOB, BUT SOMEBODY'S GOT TO DO IT.

> WATCH IT! I'M DRIVING HERE!

VEHICLES

The vehicle armada of the Empire ranges from massive, space-cruising Star Destroyers to small, one-person speeder bikes that scout and patrol the Empire's remote outposts. In between are walkers, transports, and starfighters of all shapes and sizes.

DATA FILE

- **LEADER:** EMPEROR PALPATINE
- **FOUNDED IN:** 19 BBY
- **MISSION:** TOTAL GALACTIC DOMINATION AND CONTROL

Imperial officers create strategies, win victories, and command the Empire's countless legions of stormtroopers—highly trained, elite soldiers in faceless helmets and white plastoid armor. Some Imperial troops wear gear for different environments, such as snowtroopers, who have insulated equipment for cold-weather planets.

There are many other legions of **specialized** Imperial forces, including light-armored **scout troopers** and lizard-riding **sandtroopers** for desert climates!

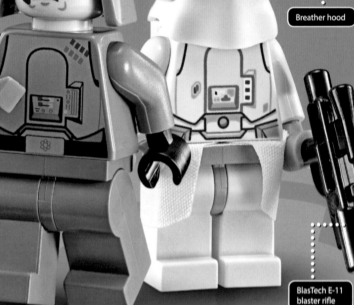

STORMTROOPER

Polarizing lenses

IMPERIAL OFFICER

SNOWTROOPER

Breather hood

Utility belt

BlasTech E-11 blaster rifle

THE DEATH STAR
With its planet-destroying superlaser, the first Death Star battle station was built to terrify the galaxy into obeying the Emperor. When it was blown up by the Rebel Alliance, the Empire started work on an even bigger and more powerful version.

TROOPER EVOLUTION
During the Clone Wars, an army of identical clone troopers fought for the Republic. Over time, their armor was upgraded from Phase I to Phase II style, and finally into the familiar stormtrooper armor of the Empire.

Phase I Clone Trooper

Phase II Clone Trooper

Imperial Stormtrooper

POWERS OF THE DARK SIDE

THE DARK SIDE promises immense knowledge and strength to those who study the ways of the Sith. It also offers special powers, many of which are forbidden to the Jedi. Here are some of the strange and dangerous abilities that Sith Lords can call upon to frighten their followers and vanquish their foes.

> TWICE THE TRAINING, TWICE THE POWER.

DOUBLE TROUBLE
Count Dooku had already gained the full skills of a Jedi Master when he joined the dark side and became Darth Tyranus. Now he is twice the threat, using all of the deadly powers at his disposal while he battles opponents with his flashing lightsaber blade.

> YIKES! IT'S GETTING A LITTLE WINDY IN HERE!

TELEKINESIS
One of Darth Vader's mightiest talents is the ability to lift objects without touching them, and then throw them through the air at his opponents. Vader uses this power against Luke Skywalker on Cloud City, battering the unsuspecting rebel with metal wreckage and smashing the large protective window behind him.

FORCE LIGHTNING
By channeling dark side energy through his body, a Sith Lord like Darth Sidious can hurl crackling electricity from his bare hands to punish or destroy those who anger him. Only a great Jedi can hope to resist this shocking power.

Some Sith Lords are so in tune with the **Force**, they can detect when an **enemy** is nearby. They can use the strength of people's **emotions** to peer into their minds and **read** their feelings!

LIGHTSABER COMBAT
A Force-sensitive warrior can predict an enemy's moves and block them with his lightsaber, or detect just the right moment to strike. When fighting someone with similar talents, a Sith like Darth Maul also uses savage surprise attacks to win the duel.

YOU'D BETTER BE.

ACK! S-SORRY I F-FORGOT YOUR BIRTHDAY, LORD VADER!

FORCE CHOKE
A common penalty for failing or displeasing Vader is the Force choke, which even works across large distances. A fortunate victim may be released if the Sith Lord is feeling merciful. As for the less fortunate ones… well, there are always more Imperial officers looking for a promotion.

REBEL ALLIANCE

ALL THE EMPEROR wants is to be the unquestioned and absolute ruler of the galaxy forever, but for some reason those pesky rebels keep interfering. They steal his secret plans, destroy his battle station, and make a nuisance of themselves at every turn. Why won't they just leave him alone?!

Traditional Alderaanian hair style

HEROES OF THE REBELLION

The Rebel Alliance is made up of beings from many worlds, all united by their desire to free the galaxy from Darth Sidious's tyranny. Anyone brave enough can join: from royalty like Princess Leia Organa, to disreputable smugglers like Han Solo.

Practical, casual smuggler's outfit

DL-44 heavy blaster pistol

HAN SOLO

DATA FILE

 LEADER: MON MOTHMA

 FOUNDED IN: 2 BBY

 MISSION: RESTORE THE GALAXY TO A REPUBLIC

REBEL HELPERS
Droids can be rebels, too. Fearless R2-D2 and always-worried C-3PO join their friends on many important missions. Without them, the Rebellion would not have found Luke Skywalker, blown up the Death Star, beaten Jabba the Hutt, or befriended the Ewoks on Endor!

> BEEP BOOP BLORP?

> NO, ARTOO, I'M NOT SURE WHAT WE'RE REBELLING AGAINST.

> " SOON THE **REBELLION** WILL BE **CRUSHED.** "
> EMPEROR PALPATINE

REBEL COMMAND
The leaders of the Rebellion are always on the run from the dark side's forces. Their hidden bases move from planet to planet and from starship to starship as they try to stay one step ahead of the Empire while thinking up strategies to defeat it.

Death Star II hologram

Rebel leader Mon Mothma

Rebel briefing room aboard the star cruiser *Home One*

> WHAT IF THIS NEW DEATH STAR IS A TRAP?

> THEN DESTROYING IT WILL BE A SNAP!

> AFTER THIS MEETING, I'LL NEED A NAP.

> DON'T WORRY, WE HAVE A MAP.

Admiral Ackbar, an amphibious Mon Calamari

Ceremonial dress for special occasions

General Crix Madine, a former Imperial officer

Newly-promoted general, Lando Calrissian

PRINCESS LEIA

REBELS OF LOTHAL
On an Outer Rim planet named Lothal, a group of determined rebels refuse to accept the new Imperial rule. Although they are vastly outnumbered by stormtroopers, Zeb, Ezra, and their fellow rebels will do anything they can to take down the Empire.

15

TAKING OVER
THE GALAXY?
PIECE OF CAKE!

GALACTIC DOMINATION

TO MOST OF ITS inhabitants, the galaxy is filled with fascinating alien worlds and cultures. But to Emperor Palpatine, every planet is just one more place to conquer in order to expand the Empire. Each planet poses unique opportunities and threats. Where will the Emperor go next?

ALDERAAN

"This mountainous world claims to be peaceful, but rumor has it that it's chock-full of rebel spies and other anti-Imperial traitors, all the way up to the royal Organa family. Still, Alderaan is a pretty place. It's a shame the planet has become such a threat to my Empire."

MISSION: Destroy at the earliest opportunity.

TATOOINE

"Ugh, Tatooine. Darth Vader tells me such horror stories about that desert planet. Too much sand for me—it's itchy and annoying and gets everywhere. Note to sandtroopers: Pack plenty of water and dewback chow."

MISSION: Avoid at all costs.

YAVIN 4

"Who lives on a moon? Apparently a bunch of people, because there are old stone pyramids all over the place. The jungles are full of bugs and other creepy-crawlies, so it's a good thing I can scare them off with the Force. Not that I'd ever go there unless it turned out to have a secret rebel base, ha ha."

MISSION: Keep an eye on Yavin 4—from a distance.

ENDOR

"A forest moon populated by harmless, fuzzy teddy bear creatures. Rumors of sophisticated tree-and-rock booby traps are probably exaggerated. This is an excellent isolated location for building the new Death Star's shield generator where no one will disturb us."

MISSION: Build generator. Minimal security necessary.

HOTH

"Frozen planets like this are why the Empire spends so many credits on cold-weather trooper gear. The ice fields may be slippery, but all-terrain walkers should be able to stomp their way across. If my robes weren't so toasty warm, I'd get chilly just looking at it!"

MISSION: Easy to conquer. Invade immediately.

BESPIN

"A gas giant of interest only to miners and get-rich-quick types. The Cloud City mining outpost that floats above it is of little importance, but might be worth making an example of to ensure nobody else thinks they're beyond the Empire's reach. A detachment of stormtroopers should be sufficient."

MISSION: Show them who's boss.

CORUSCANT

"The Imperial Center—my official headquarters (when I'm not vacationing on the Death Star). No one threatens the Empire's seat of power, thanks to all of the stormtroopers and Royal Guards stationed here."

MISSION: Continue with top-level security operation. And keep an eye out for anyone in a brown-hooded robe hanging around the abandoned Jedi Temple.

HOW DO YOU KEEP an entire galaxy in line? If you're Darth Sidious, you build a moon-sized battle station capable of blowing up an entire planet with a single blast. Sure, it might be a little extreme, but it's guaranteed to stop the citizens of your Empire from complaining all the time!

The Death Star took about **20 years** to build… and about **20 minutes** for rebel pilot Luke Skywalker to **destroy!**

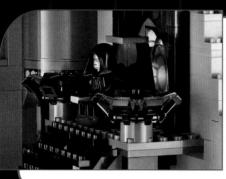

THRONE ROOM
Wherever he goes, the Emperor always wants to be in control. All of his palaces, command ships, and even the Death Star itself are equipped with throne rooms from where he can give orders and watch over his Empire.

TIE FIGHTER HANGARS
Just in case any troublesome rebels come calling, the Death Star's hangars hold about 7,000 TIE fighters ready for battle. When needed, these ships drop down from ceiling-mounted storage racks and launch out into space.

BRIDGE SHAFT
The Death Star is not entirely pedestrian-friendly. It is full of deep shafts and chasms, with only narrow retracting bridges to let its occupants cross. If a bridge fails to deploy, then good luck —better hope you have a grappling hook on you!

DEATH STAR 1
The original Death Star is 75 miles (120 km) across, with a disc-shaped focusing lens for its devastatingly powerful superlaser. The Emperor thinks it is indestructible, but a tiny thermal exhaust port proves to be

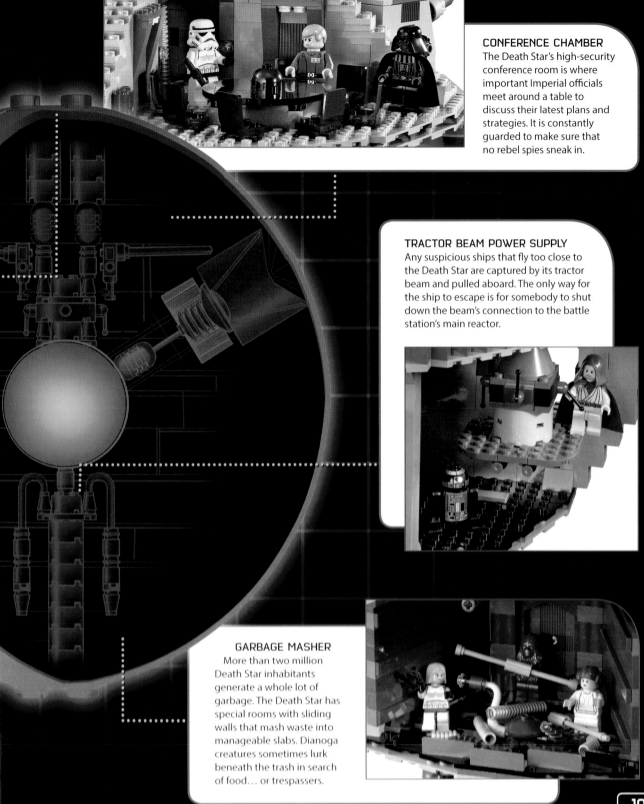

CONFERENCE CHAMBER
The Death Star's high-security conference room is where important Imperial officials meet around a table to discuss their latest plans and strategies. It is constantly guarded to make sure that no rebel spies sneak in.

TRACTOR BEAM POWER SUPPLY
Any suspicious ships that fly too close to the Death Star are captured by its tractor beam and pulled aboard. The only way for the ship to escape is for somebody to shut down the beam's connection to the battle station's main reactor.

GARBAGE MASHER
More than two million Death Star inhabitants generate a whole lot of garbage. The Death Star has special rooms with sliding walls that mash waste into manageable slabs. Dianoga creatures sometimes lurk beneath the trash in search of food… or trespassers.

OBI-WAN KENOBI

ONCE, OBI-WAN KENOBI was Anakin Skywalker's teacher and best friend, but that ended when Anakin became Darth Vader. Obi-Wan went into hiding after the Jedi were defeated, and Vader has never been able to find him. When they meet again on the Death Star, Vader finally has his chance for revenge.

Darth Vader never guessed that his enemy **Obi-Wan** was living on Anakin Skywalker's own **home planet** of **Tatooine!**

Hangar bay entrance

Millennium Falcon in hangar bay

I HAVE THE STRANGEST SENSE OF DÉJÀ VU.

YOU TOO?

Retracted blast door

DEATH STAR DUEL

Vader senses Obi-Wan's presence aboard the Empire's secret battle station and confronts him. They duel with lightsabers, but Obi-Wan disappears as Vader strikes the finishing blow, becoming one with the Force.

66 IF YOU **STRIKE** ME DOWN, I SHALL BECOME MORE **POWERFUL** THAN YOU CAN POSSIBLY IMAGINE. 99

OBI-WAN KENOBI

FORMER ALLIES

Obi-Wan has known Anakin Skywalker since Anakin was very young. As Jedi partners, they shared many adventures. Obi-Wan always knew that Anakin was reckless and overconfident, but he never dreamed that his apprentice might fall to the dark side.

Gray hair

Old Jedi robes double as hermit disguise

Rarely used lightsaber

ON VACATION

Obi-Wan was one of the hardest-working Jedi Knights, but his life wasn't all fighting Sith, foiling Separatist plots, and instructing his rebellious Padawan. Between missions, Obi-Wan liked to kick back and relax by the pool on the peaceful planet Alderaan.

LIFE IN EXILE

As one of the few Jedi to survive the Clone Wars, Obi-Wan fled to Tatooine. Disguised as a desert hermit known as "Old Ben" Kenobi, he has spent the years watching over Anakin's son, Luke, waiting for the day when he can train the boy in the Force.

DATA FILE

- **HOMEWORLD:** STEWJON
- **BIRTH DATE:** 57 BBY
-  **RANK:** JEDI MASTER
-  **TRAINED BY:** QUI-GON JINN
- 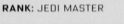 **WEAPON:** BLUE-BLADED LIGHTSABER

IMPERIAL FLEET

IT'S A COLORFUL galaxy out there… and Darth Sidious doesn't like that one bit. That's why he builds his Empire's fleet in orderly shades of black, white, and lots of gray. It gives everything a nice, unified look, and it makes his ships so much easier to keep clean.

SUPER STAR DESTROYER
Darth Vader's gargantuan battle cruiser.
SIZE 12 miles (19 km) long
SPEED 40 megalight (MGLT)
CAPACITY 320,000 crew and personnel
WEAPONS Turbolaser batteries, ion cannons, laser cannons, concussion missiles

Intimidating dagger shape

Command bridge tower

STAR DESTROYER
Massive, mile-long warships.
SIZE 1 mile (1.6 km) long
SPEED 60 MGLT
CAPACITY 47,000 crew and personnel
WEAPONS Turbolaser turrets, ion cannons

Solar array wing

Turbolaser turret

Transparisteel viewport

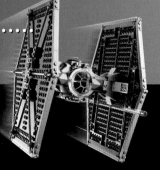

TIE FIGHTER
Standard twin ion engine combat starfighter.
SIZE 29.5 feet (8.99 m) long
SPEED 100 MGLT
CAPACITY 1 pilot
WEAPONS 2 laser cannons

TIE INTERCEPTOR
A faster and deadlier version of the TIE fighter.
SIZE 31.5 feet (9.6 m) long
SPEED 111 MGLT
CAPACITY 1 pilot
WEAPONS 4 laser cannons

TIE ADVANCED
Darth Vader's prototype personal starfighter.
SIZE 30 feet (9.2 m) long
SPEED 105 MGLT
CAPACITY 1 pilot
WEAPONS 2 laser cannons, cluster missiles

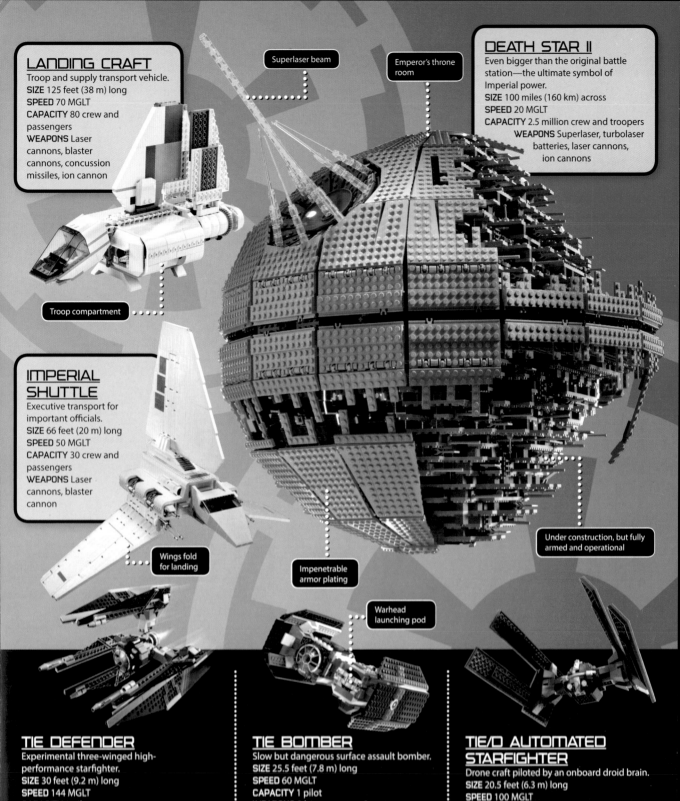

LANDING CRAFT
Troop and supply transport vehicle.
SIZE 125 feet (38 m) long
SPEED 70 MGLT
CAPACITY 80 crew and
passengers
WEAPONS Laser
cannons, blaster
cannons, concussion
missiles, ion cannon

Superlaser beam

Emperor's throne room

DEATH STAR II
Even bigger than the original battle
station—the ultimate symbol of
Imperial power.
SIZE 100 miles (160 km) across
SPEED 20 MGLT
CAPACITY 2.5 million crew and troopers
WEAPONS Superlaser, turbolaser
batteries, laser cannons,
ion cannons

Troop compartment

IMPERIAL SHUTTLE
Executive transport for
important officials.
SIZE 66 feet (20 m) long
SPEED 50 MGLT
CAPACITY 30 crew and
passengers
WEAPONS Laser
cannons, blaster
cannon

Wings fold
for landing

Impenetrable
armor plating

Under construction, but fully
armed and operational

Warhead
launching pod

TIE DEFENDER
Experimental three-winged high-
performance starfighter.
SIZE 30 feet (9.2 m) long
SPEED 144 MGLT
CAPACITY 1 pilot
WEAPONS 4 laser cannons, 2 ion cannons,
2 warhead launchers

TIE BOMBER
Slow but dangerous surface assault bomber.
SIZE 25.5 feet (7.8 m) long
SPEED 60 MGLT
CAPACITY 1 pilot
WEAPONS 2 laser cannons, 2 proton
torpedo launchers, 2 concussion missile
launchers, bomb bay

TIE/D AUTOMATED STARFIGHTER
Drone craft piloted by an onboard droid brain.
SIZE 20.5 feet (6.3 m) long
SPEED 100 MGLT
CAPACITY None
WEAPONS 2 laser cannons

LUKE SKYWALKER

ANAKIN SKYWALKER'S SON, Luke, is hidden from his father on Tatooine, where he grows up as a farm boy far from the reach of the Empire and the dark side. When he is drawn into the galactic conflict, Luke joins forces with the rebels. He must quickly learn to be a Jedi… before he faces Darth Vader himself!

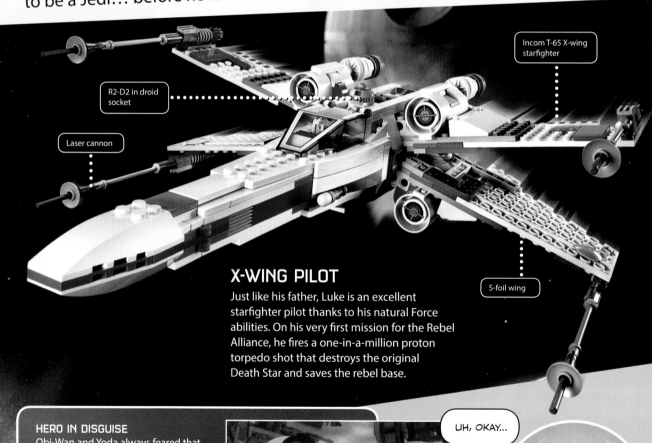

R2-D2 in droid socket

Incom T-65 X-wing starfighter

Laser cannon

S-foil wing

X-WING PILOT

Just like his father, Luke is an excellent starfighter pilot thanks to his natural Force abilities. On his very first mission for the Rebel Alliance, he fires a one-in-a-million proton torpedo shot that destroys the original Death Star and saves the rebel base.

HERO IN DISGUISE

Obi-Wan and Yoda always feared that Luke might follow in Anakin's footsteps, but this isn't what they had in mind! Chased by his fans, Luke puts on a cheap Darth Vader costume and somehow ends up in command of a squad of Imperial troops.

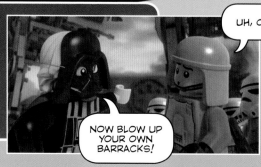

UH, OKAY...

NOW BLOW UP YOUR OWN BARRACKS!

Obi-Wan didn't tell **Luke** much about his father. All Luke knew was that **Anakin Skywalker** was a great Jedi Knight… and that he had been destroyed by **Darth Vader!**

Green-bladed lightsaber

A DARK WARNING
As part of Luke's Jedi training, his Master, Yoda, sends him into a cave that is strong with the dark side. Inside, Luke faces a vision of Darth Vader that transforms into Luke himself—a sign of what could be his own destiny… if he isn't careful.

MONSTER BATTLE
Luke's Jedi training has equipped him with quick wits and even faster reflexes. When he comes face to face with Jabba the Hutt's rancor beast, Luke has to act fast. He wedges a large bone into the rancor's mouth, giving himself time to escape.

Glove covers robotic hand

DATA FILE
 HOMEWORLD: TATOOINE
 BIRTH DATE: 19 BBY
 RANK: JEDI KNIGHT
 TAUGHT BY: OBI-WAN KENOBI, YODA
 WEAPON: BLUE- AND LATER GREEN-BLADED LIGHTSABER

SITH OR JEDI?
Luke's headstrong nature and natural Force powers make him a perfect candidate for a new Sith apprentice. Darth Sidious wants to recruit him to replace Darth Vader, but Luke is determined to bring Vader back to the side of good instead.

> **"I AM A JEDI, LIKE MY FATHER BEFORE ME."**
> LUKE SKYWALKER

Black fighting clothes

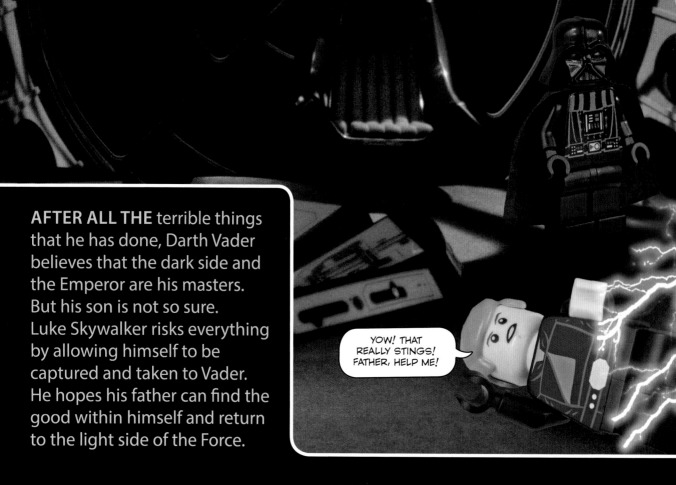

AFTER ALL THE terrible things that he has done, Darth Vader believes that the dark side and the Emperor are his masters. But his son is not so sure. Luke Skywalker risks everything by allowing himself to be captured and taken to Vader. He hopes his father can find the good within himself and return to the light side of the Force.

YOW! THAT REALLY STINGS! FATHER, HELP ME!

CAN A SITH LORD

THAT'S IT, VADER. YOU'RE FIRED!

THE FINAL SITH
As Darth Vader sees his son in danger, something awakens deep inside him. He seizes the Emperor and hurls him down the Death Star's reactor shaft. Darth Sidious is no more—but his Sith lightning has damaged Vader's life-support systems.

LIGHTNING STRIKE

Vader is a remorseless Sith Lord, yet he still feels a connection to his son. Vader brings Luke to the Emperor aboard the second Death Star, but Luke refuses to turn to the dark side. In a rage, the Emperor attacks him with deadly Force lightning! Vader's feelings about Luke grow stronger, and he wonders whether a part of Anakin remains alive after all.

NEVER GONNA HAPPEN, KID!

By destroying the **Emperor** once and for all, Anakin finally fulfills the **prophecy** that said he would one day bring **balance** to the **Force.**

BE REDEEMED?

FROM SITH TO JEDI
Darth Vader has lived under a mask for 23 years. Reunited with the light side of the Force, he asks Luke to remove his helmet so he can see out of Anakin's eyes once more. Anakin passes on, asking Luke to tell Leia that Luke was right about their father's goodness all along.

ONE WITH THE FORCE
When a noble Jedi departs from the physical world, he becomes one with the Force. As Luke burns Vader's armor on a pyre on the forest moon of Endor, he sees the spirits of three old friends: Obi-Wan Kenobi, Yoda, and Anakin Skywalker—Jedi Knight.

GLOSSARY

CLONE WARS
A series of galaxy-wide battles fought between the Republic's Clone Army and the Separatist Droid Army, which took place between 22 and 19 BBY.

CORUSCANT
The capital of the Republic—and later, the Empire. This planet is home to the Senate and the Jedi Temple.

CYBERNETIC
Something that is half mechanical, half biological.

CYBORG
A being that is partly a living organism and partly a robot.

DEATH STAR
An enormous Imperial battle station, which has enough firepower to destroy an entire planet.

EMPEROR
Ruler of the Empire.

EMPIRE
A tyrannical power that rules the galaxy under the leadership of Emperor Palpatine, a Sith Lord.

FORCE
The energy that flows through all living things. It can be used for good or evil.

FORCE LIGHTNING
Deadly rays of blue energy used as a weapon.

JEDI
A member of the Jedi Order who studies the light side of the Force.

JEDI KNIGHT
A full member of the Jedi Order who has completed his or her training.

JEDI MASTER
An experienced and high-ranking Jedi who has demonstrated great skill and dedication.

JEDI ORDER
An ancient organization that promotes peace and justice throughout the galaxy.

JEDI TEMPLE
The headquarters of the Jedi Order, located on the planet Coruscant.

LIGHTSABER
A sword-like weapon with a blade of pure energy that is used by Jedi and Sith.

PADAWAN
A young Jedi apprentice who is in training to become a fully fledged Jedi Knight.

REBEL ALLIANCE
The organization that resists and fights the Empire.

REPUBLIC
The democratic government that rules many planets in the galaxy.

SITH
An ancient sect of Force-sensitives who seek to use the dark side of the Force to gain power.

DK | Penguin Random House

Editors	**Shari Last and Matt Jones**
Designers	**Jon Hall and Rhys Thomas**
Additional Designers	**Julie Thompson and Mark Richards**
Senior DTP Designer	**David McDonald**
Senior Producer	**Lloyd Robertson**
Managing Editor	**Simon Hugo**
Design Manager	**Guy Harvey**
Creative Manager	**Sarah Harland**
Art Director	**Lisa Lanzarini**
Publisher	**Julie Ferris**
Publishing Director	**Simon Beecroft**

Additional photography by Gary Ombler.

Dorling Kindersley would like to thank Randi Sørensen and Robert Stefan Ekblom
at the LEGO Group; Jonathan W. Rinzler, Troy Alders, Rayne Roberts, Pablo Hidalgo,
and Leland Chee at Lucasfilm; and Jo Casey for editorial assistance.

First published in the United States in 2015 by
DK Publishing, 345 Hudson Street, New York, New York, 10014

Contains material previously published in LEGO® *Star Wars*®: The Dark Side (2014)

002-284485-Feb/15

Page design copyright © 2015 Dorling Kindersley Limited
A Penguin Random House Company

LEGO, the LEGO logo, the Brick and Knob configurations, and the Minifigure are
trademarks of the LEGO Group
© 2015 the LEGO Group.
Produced by Dorling Kindersley under license from the LEGO Group.

© & TM 2015 LUCASFILM LTD.

A catalog record for this book is available from the
Library of Congress.

ISBN: 978-5-0010-1302-0

Color reproduction by Alta Image, UK
Printed and bound in China

www.dk.com
www.LEGO.com/starwars
www.starwars.com

A WORLD OF IDEAS:
SEE ALL THERE IS TO KNOW